"We have a mirror for our souls in remembering
holy men and women,
and recounting their blessed life history.
In this mirror you will behold the blemishes,
which will disfigure your soul."

SAINT CHRYSOSTOM

MOTHER

BLESSED MOTHER

THE STORY OF A GIRL NAMED AGNES

Hubert Robin Gomez

Rupa . Co

Published 2004 by
Rupa & Co
7/16, Ansari Road, Daryaganj
New Delhi 110 002

Sales Centres:
Allahabad Bangalore Chandigarh Chennai
Hyderabad Jaipur Kathmandu
Kolkata Ludhiana Mumbai Pune

Illustrations by the author

Designed & typeset by
Arrt Creations
45 Nehru Apts, Kalkaji
New Delhi 110 019

Printed in India by
Gopsons Paper Ltd
A-14 Sector 60
Noida 201 301

In loving remembrance of
Mother
who taught me how to love
God's Children

And for Elizabeth,
my mother

And
Dhukhi Ram, Fatima, Mary Bella

And finally, for
Sita, John, Ramesh, Vijay, Carmel, Rebecca, Santosh
and many more whom I have not met, but know
that through the love and devotion of a single person,
they are living a better life

Contents

Foreword

AS a thoroughbred Calcuttan, our city and our people always played an important role in my life. One such person was Mother Teresa, a neighbour of our locality. It was way back in the early 1960s, when I was twelve, that I met her with my mother at our Church, St Teresa of Avila, on Lower Circular Road opposite the Entally Market. Those were the days when the Missionaries of Charity had not achieved such magnitude or fame; it was a free mixing of a handful of Nuns and Sisters as Mother was in the process of building an institution through her vision of Faith, Hope and Charity.

I met her quite often at our Church where she and her Sisters used to come to attend mass and a friendship of sorts grew between them and our family. They had this relationship with practically all the other parishioners in our locality and each family did whatever they could afford in their own little way for her cause. I used to go to Shishu Bhavan, which was next door along with my mother quite often to help the Sisters with their chores. Whether it was to feed the poor of Taltolla and Beniapukur with "kichree", wash the nappies and bedsheets of the abandoned babies that were taken care of at Shishu Bhavan, or distribute blankets, cake and cookies and some more kichree during Christmas time, it was always a worthwhile experience.

Our years grew and so did Mother's and her work. During those years my education led me to start a career and also pursue a hobby that was solely self-taught, and many sketches were done of the "Angels in blue bordered white saris," looking after the poor, the sick, the dying and also at prayer. My visits to Shishu Bhavan dropped considerably because of my work schedule but her presence was always alive through my rough sketches accompanied by small notes about her.

I would often see her scurrying past in her white Peugeot car, a frail figure clutching a blue cloth bag with wooden handles, a smile on her face, and a rosary in her hand. Her mission led her to various places and her work was followed by me with great interest as they were constantly reported by the media. And, most of the time, I was agog with wonder as to how such a small woman could achieve what she did. The answer was there all the time. Her Faith, her Hope, her Charity were all that were needed to serve mankind. And, she was enthusiastic about God. For, she did not once hesitate to ask Him for the Graces which He offers to all. And, she asked Him well. In her prayers, in her self-styled hermetic life and above all, her constant movement that demonstrated how she felt for the poor and the afflicted. Meeting people at high and low places. Meeting kings and nobility, Presidents, Ministers and Government officials for a little piece of land, a kind word, a small gesture, always willing to face any situation, the more difficult the better with faith that gave her strength.

Mother is no longer with us and I for one miss her diminutive figure, her milky white smile and creases all over her face. I miss her stern commands to her Sisters, her clipped rather stony utterance of the English language with a few broken words in Bengali and Hindi shoved in, her hurried walk and oneness with Christ, in her genuflection. Many, like me, miss her too and our glimpse of this sense of loss is rewarded by what she has left behind. And, for us to follow. In her unhesitating, extraordinary and often miraculously healing nature of comforting.

I have often thought of sharing my experiences by writing about her and her amazing talent of conviction, sincerity, passion and fervour of her call, but dismissed the idea as many have written about her and it could have been described as yet another biographical compilation. But a nagging strain of incompleteness always remained which translated itself into writing after I saw my rather immature sketches long forgotten, but very well preserved by my mother, though yellowing with age and totally unprofessional in style and attitude. A few spelling mistakes in the accompanied notes brought back memories of another day, as if that small sari-clad figure was in front of me and the beginning of the first draft slowly materialized.

I did have the opportunity to read many an author describing Mother and her work and I have gained through their in-depth narration. But what persuaded me to write on seeing the long-forgotten sketches of a child was something that I had read, said by St Paul, "We are all fellow-citizens of the Saints. In fact, the Saints are part of our family—our ancestors. We can have a spiritual family tree, and what is more, we may choose our own favourites, our ideals! This is a family album of our wonderful relatives in the universal Catholic family." And, how true St Paul was. Mother is definitely a part of my family album and one of my favourites.

This is neither a biography nor a fictionalized account, but a deep heartfelt gratitude of a man who knew her during his formative years, which have had a lasting impression. As also a matter-of-fact look into the mind of that girl sitting beside the fireplace in their small house in Skopje, or watching the pristine beauty of Kanchenjunga or even the wasteland near Topsia and Tiljala and what could have gone on in her mind at the age of twelve or twenty or at forty, contemplating her next move to bring a better world for the downtrodden. And, the three persons who will always be thankful of her caring. I have met these three and I met them many years after as well, when their life was entwined with Mother's.

What you may find is not the familiarity of Mother's life and times which today are known to many, but the virtual mirror of a soul who received happiness and the strength to live, which it is hoped may bring other points of interest and some delightful surprises.

In trying to undertake a task of such universal proportions, I discussed and consulted with some of the elders in our locality who had not only worked for the Missionaries of Charity full-time, but also some who became personal friends of Mother. Having had an experience of my own, though in my childhood and teenage years, I decided to include a few interesting and instructive facts, and of course, the phenomenon of how this extraordinary person from a strange land with strange looks conquered, in an alien nation, with an alien tongue, alien colour and alien climate.

The sincerity of her goal was utterly different from many other saintly lives, and what one single God-loving soul could achieve became a worldwide phenomenon. Her Tabernacles of Love in every possible country on Mother Earth is a testament of immense self-sacrifice. Of prudence and of pious self, worthy of credence.

From the sleepy village of Skopje, to the flowing dales of Ireland, to the foothills of the Himalayan Mountains, from continent to continent this very small and frail wrinkled woman transformed the meaning of love and caring. And, that woman became a universal Mother. A Mother of love. Of superb courage born out of Faith, Hope and Charity.

This is the story about Agnes. And the three, who from the jaws of death resurrected to a new life.

I am grateful for having met her, for having touched her feet in greeting, for her hand on my head in blessing and for having partook of the many meals at Shishu Bhavan. For, coming to know that to see into a mirror, is to behold the blemishes of one's own soul. That somewhere in the world around us some forgotten soul is saved, fed, clothed and given a decent burial. That a single human being could change our lives.

That I met a Saint when I was a lad of twelve.

Hubert Robin Gomez
Calcutta. June 2003.

Of Agnes

Her mind was made up, and Agnes's life changed radically forever. She had a goal now, and all her energies poured into achieving it. She'd think later about exactly how to go to India, that distant land that beckoned her; right now she had to get ready to go to Ireland. And she went. She went to Ireland.

And, she came to India. To a place called Calcutta.

Where she met Hell. A hell that gave her a Heaven.

She also went to Tanzania, and to Rome. She went to Nagasaki, she went to Colombo, she went to Tabora, she went to Caracas, and she went to Brouke, an Aborigine centre in Australia, and to Melbourne. She also went to Amman in Jordan. And, by the time she was sixty years old she had gone to all the corners of the world opening doors, bringing light to a world that was sightless, dark and cruel. A world that was rejected by the very world it lived in.

She went to hell and made a heaven for them. A heaven full of love and caring, compassion and self-esteem so that they could live a life with dignity and self-respect. She gave our world a vocation. A vocation which men, women, young people and children alike from all religious denominations took up to serve the poorest of the poor, cutting across caste, colour and creed in the spirit of prayer and sacrifice.

Her desire to create this paradise was from the very teachings of Christ Himself:

"For I was hungered, and ye gave me to eat:
I was thirsty, and ye gave me drink:
I was a stranger, and ye took me in:
Naked and ye clothed me:
I was in prison, and ye came unto me....
Inasmuch as ye have done it unto one of the least of my brethren,
Ye have done it unto me."

The poor became her children, the deprived her companions, the hungry her soul-mates, the afflicted her concern, the needy her support and encouragement, and with a constant prayer on her lips she went on unabated. "Make us worthy Lord, to serve our fellow-men throughout the world that live and die in poverty and hunger. Give them through our hands, this day their daily bread, and by our understanding love give peace and joy."

Her approach was as simple as her upbringing itself–of pure, wholehearted commitment.

In recognizing God in the person of the poor. In loving God better through works of charity and serving the poor. In worshipping God through prayer and sacrifice. In finding God by keeping the family spirit kindled.

And, in giving to God the greatest sacrifice of all, of oneself.

An Act of Faith

Faith, the supreme guide of one's soul gives in each one of us the confidence and the conviction of belief. After all, if our parents told us to do something or not to do it, wouldn't we listen to them? Similarly, the Acts of Faith are gestures of trust, of belief interwoven with the spirit of adoration.

The basics of Christianity are wrapped around this synthesis of firm belief. It is this theme that evokes stronly the distinct language, that is called 'Faith.' The intimacy between oneself and Christ. For, with Faith, you are in the physical and material composition in the humanity of God in His glorified self.

Either you have Faith in believing this or you don't, but the Acts of Faith are a continuous process of the Truth and the Source of all Truths received from Christ. To understand its genuine sense, all of us just have to see what Mother has placed in the organic body of time and space.

Mother's conviction to adore and firmly believe that through Faith and Baptism she was incorporated into Christ, shows us that the Christian with Christ dies to rise again to a new life. Her immense Faith has shown us that someone who was dying in life, itself arose to live again.

This is an Act of Faith.

FAITH

Lord, make me a channel of Thy peace...

Meet Dhukhi Ram

HIS name was Arjun Krishna Dhukhi Ram. Five feet two inches tall and weighing 45 kg. A native aboriginal from the district of Hazaribagh, from the Adivasi tribe in the state of Bihar, a princely kingdom once upon a time. A Hindu, a husband, father, tiller of the land and part-time burial assistant in providing firewood to the master of ceremonies from the forest that surrounded his shanty, in the bustee of Mahanagar fifteen km away from the main town. He was illiterate, underweight and suffering from whooping cough and other congenital ailments that wracked his chest and his innards. He had other problems as well. He could not feed his two daughters and his twenty-eight-year-old wife, the latter an illiterate and a bulldozing woman whose forehead and forearms were tattooed with dots and dashes. A star and a circle on the centre of her throat and the collarbone from where all her sound of fury arose. Her voice was always hoarse from smoking the roasted leaves of the *sal* tree stuffed with heady ganja, which grew freely in those parts.

Arjun Krishna Dhukhi Ram had a problem, a problem that was shared by the very many like him. But he did not know how to tackle it. His meagre salary of two hundred rupees per month couldn't sustain the demands of his family and himself. He was overworked and always taken for a ride. And his wife, a horrendous being of loathsome vulgarity, always abused Dhukhi for his shortcomings. Dhukhi, as he was fondly called by his long-since forgotten parents prayed for an end to his life of misery. He was bent double by the load of firewood and his miserable self, and he wanted the shortest route to oblivion, as he lay resting in the open fields and sometimes under the shade of the *sal* tree. Or, sometimes in the open besides his shanty, looking up at the stars and the moon when it was there, wondering who he was and what had befell him.

Dhukhi chose the short-cut to end his life's problems. He went that moonless night to the pond not so far away, tied a rope around his leg, with the other end fastened to a huge boulder, and with all his remaining strength, waded the waters to sink thirty-five feet below to his death.

Dhukhi Ram did not die. He was rescued by his bustee folk, who hearing the calls of a submerged spirit half-choked in his own sputum and the dirty water and suffocated by his own lungi. Poor chap, he did not even have a vest to dress up for his own funeral. They pulled and they dragged, some even trying to hack his leg off with the boulder, which eventually came off and saved his life, thanks to his crematorium bully, who wanted to show his compassion and forgiveness for all the half-paid dues for the firewood carrier. This man was known as Bhoot Ram.

Dhukhi survived and lived in fits and starts at a government dispensary, as hospitals were few and far in between, on a diet of water and ground pulses, which in any case was the staple diet of the region. He was sinking with every passing second, and what lay beneath the soiled counterpane was a skeleton of human disregard.

It was Bhoot Ram who again came to his assistance with a few rupees. He shifted this wretched bundle of skin and bones to a hospital in Calcutta.

Arjun Krishna Dhukhi Ram, faceless and redundant, did not know that his name also consisted of a few names of gods. Always being called Dhukhi, 'The Pitiful', from his birth, he did not even know that these heavenly bodies made up his name. For, whence he was being admitted, his entry in the record book showed thus. None of his namesakes descended to help him.

Dhukhi spent his waking hours in extreme pain; his right leg, knee downwards took a gangrenous beating and his coughing never stopped. He became a burden to the ward staff who took the easy way out, of stuffing a ball of opium into his mouth so that the delirium ended, to be repeated again when he regained consciousness. This carried on for a few weeks and ultimately his cries drew the sympathy of the warden. The doctors were consulted and his right leg was operated upon.

He woke up one day to find that he was still alive and in pain, and half his leg missing. The wail of his agony could be heard throughout the fifteen-acre colonial buildings and sprawling lawns. His cry could be felt by the waters of the tanks surrounding the hospital, for they shimmered in unison, cry after cry. The rafters shook, the crows fled. Dhukhi prayed for an end to his misery. His prayers were answered

A small frail sari-clad woman in her fifties, visiting the hospitals around the city, as was her practice, touched his head and healed him.

The Call

The introduction was very direct and had a bit of foreboding, for I did not know who she was, when I heard my mother say, "Touch her feet." I did as I was told and on getting up I felt her hands on my head with a smile on her face. "Jisū prōnam, Māāther." "Jisū prōnam, and what is your name?" Before I could reply my mother announced, "his name is Robin, and he is a very naughty boy. Does not study, always painting and drawing, wants to become an artist. Please, bless him properly Mother, so that he can pass his exams."

I was embarrassed at what my mother said, especially to someone I did not know and a foreigner. She said something in passing which I did not hear, being a bit red around the ears. But kneeling besides my mother in the church I saw her from the corner of my eye, an image that has stayed with me till today.

What I saw was a picture of concentration in prayer. There was a mystique about her. Her stance, her appearance. The pale, craggy-lined face and the white sari with blue borders, with another white piece of cloth under it, neatly kept in place with two pins. Hands folded with a slightly large wooden rosary, eyes closed, lips moving clutching the wooden cross at the end of the rosary with all her strength, was something that I never saw before. I was a regular churchgoer, have seen a lot of people praying and meditating, but such expression of prayer was never seen by me before. And, I wondered, that this lady sure had something very important to ask from God. She surely did, which I came to know when I started to visit Shishu Bhavan with my mother.

That evening, I did a small sketch of what I saw in Church, with a small caption at the bottom, which said, "Mother's prayer..."

Shishu Bhavan was just two streets away from our house in Entally. A non-descript concrete structure with a big imposing gate in the front. My going to Shishu Bhavan was very convenient after school in the early evenings and especially on Thursdays when our school was closed. This became a regular feature and saying "going to Shishu Bhavan" made life a lot simpler, especially with the homework that needed to be done. But my mother understood the design of my purpose and once or twice I felt guilty, for, I could make out that Mother also knew. I did my homework. And, I went to Shishu Bhavan, and I asked my mother a lot of questions. Questions from a young mind that was of top priority. Who was she? Where did she come from? What is she doing here?, and so on. What I came to know was extremely informative and enlightening.

Mother, I was told, came from a far away country called Yugoslavia. Born in the year 1910 to Albanian parents and named Agnes, she also had a brother and a sister. She attended the local government school and was a member of the Sodality Group, from where her mission and call emerged.

During that time, some local Jesuit Yugoslav priests took the long journey to India and attached themselves to the Bengal mission under the Archdiocese of Calcutta. These ecclesiastical clerics away from home used to write to their families and to their local church about their work and the various places that they visited. One of them went to Kurseong, a beautiful hill station in the foothills of the Himalayas in Bengal, and his letters captured the young Agnes's interest.

She opted to volunteer for the cause. And, she went to Ireland to join the Loreto nuns, as they were also working in the Archdiocese of Calcutta.

Agnes prepared herself for the long journey to Ireland. The subject of her going to such a faraway place was discussed many times; India, but in stony silence she revealed her intention. She had to go. She has been called to go.

Every Christian family has the desire that at least one offspring of theirs should go to serve the Holy Mother the Church, and this deliberation comes from the Christian way of life, of a promise made to God of a free, supererogatory good. Our lives, from our childhood, has always been around these feelings that one day the call will come to serve our Master.

We too, had a Sodality group in our school, and it was not so difficult to understand the nature in which Agnes left her home to come to such a faraway place and make it her home. But my young brain thought it otherwise. Does a bell ring in the mind, does someone catch your hand and take you to the railway station or does someone give you a push and you leave? But slowly I understood the meaning of that call.

Vocations of the religious kind are totally an interior phenomenon, there is no corresponding reality present that can be perceived by the five senses, and when it takes place you just pack up your bags and go.

In our neighbourhood such calls were many, my elder sister's school friend and her brother, my two buddies from Krishnanagar, my classmate's elder brother, and even my own younger brother. The call to serve the church comes at an early age and these young ones leave their family to join the seminaries and noviciates to prepare themselves for celibate life thereafter. Some pursue their vision to serve God, others wander and some fail, finding it too difficult to live such an austere life. Agnes's vocation was no different than the others that I knew. She also had a loving family, a happy home, affectionate grandparents, giggly schoolmates and all the fun and frolic associated with a young girl. She also chose to be one with Christ, but there was a difference in her call. The difference lay in what we see today.

Agnes, I was told, went to join the Loreto Abbey in Rathfarnham, Dublin in Ireland, when she was eighteen years old, from there she came to the noviciate at Darjeeling, in West Bengal. After few years she went to Calcutta and started teaching geography at St Mary's High School, and for some years she was also the principal. She was in charge of the Daughters of St Anne, a religious order attached to the Loreto Sisters. During this time, her decision to leave the Loreto House and take up a small tenement at Entally was sent to Rome and was approved. Sister Agnes's meeting with the stupendous paradox that was Calcutta, had begun.

The authority of promises and fulfilment of any kind lies in the guarantee of providing. The fulfilment and prophecy of such spirit with God has been given to us, and, the fulfilment of sharing with the Almighty what life is, was chosen by Agnes as a pleader for mankind. What Agnes saw was the gladness that she could bring. For, the most vivid expectations of the hope in the living became her fundamental, human promise. The promise of providing.

She became what she is today, we aren't.

Her Faith gave her entrance into the invisible realities, which are the substance of what mankind hopes for. Christ has brought about the redemption of the world and through baptism, the Christian becomes a sharer in that redemption. The decision of Christ to bring all to definite salvation is irrevocable; salvation, however, can only happen between people with freedom, the freedom of God in self-gift and the freedom of the Christian in the continued reception of that gift. This pilgrimage of faith can only be fully attainable through hope. In hope we are saved, but hope will not be hope, if its object is seen, and hoping for what we cannot see means awaiting with patient endurance.

Our emphasis on the hopes may lead us to abandonment of the world's present crises. The present life is also not a theatre where trials and tribulations are mixed with conscious theories. For, a great act of giving is a new heaven in an old earth, a place created out of love where righteousness abounds. Agnes, through Christ, renewed the spirit, so that the poor, the afflicted and the downtrodden live again through His mystical body and embrace once and for all the redemptive act: The act of Love.

The authority of Mother among men and women of supreme talent neither diminishes nor stops with time. It grows. The familiarity of her work neither stales our delight nor reduces our wonder as to its variety. Her mind and her talent is seen with amazement throughout the world as the work of an exceptional architect. Her conquering power is visible in every step that we take. Not only in Calcutta but all over the world. A hill is easily surveyed than a mountain whose total height, indeed, may never be visible to us at any time. But Mother saw all around it. Her faith revealed to us a new exploration, her zeal revealed succession of amazement, and her singular purpose have touched our mind, our heart and our soul, with love arising from respect to submission.

This was the Mother that I came to know, refecting a vivid awareness of life around us. Of suffering that brought tolerance. Of endurance that brought determination. And, out of determination, hope. The trials through which we triumph.

The name Shishu Bhavan describes what it stands for, that of a house for children. Initially, going to Shishu Bhavan was a big event, of meeting the Sisters and helping them. Sometimes with a ladle, sometimes pumping the handle of the tube well drawing water, and sometimes washing as well. The Sisters, from all across the country and some from overseas, were a happy, cheerful lot. Always smiling with a few words of pleasantries, and some of them became my friends irrespective of our age differences.

There was Sister Mary Joseph, the chef. Sister Bernadette, the musician. Sister Beatrice, the seamstress and Sister Rosalyn from Italy, the cobbler. I was amazed at their mastery in what they did. The food, however simple was delicious. The music and the choir were heavenly. The sewing machines churned out pillow cases and bed sheets and the walking shoes were well looked after with all the tools of the trade by Sister Rosalyn the cobbler.

And they walked everywhere. In twos and threes. Sixes and nines, and sometimes in a group as if in a procession, always reciting the rosary. Traffic stopped whenever they crossed the streets; policemen were not necessary for any motorist to see this sight and stop. Their journey was to all the lanes of Calcutta. Picking up a rickety child, being summoned to hospitals to rescue a newborn without a mother, collecting babies abandoned in garbage dumps and sometime at their own doorstep. And, all of them were given shelter at Shishu Bhavan, a home specially made for them by Mother.

This business of children been abandoned was something that I could not comprehend and often asked the question, why should a newborn or a few-days-old gift from God be left alone in the streets to die? The question was answered many years later by myself when I grew up. But to see the Sisters in the daily work was truly a wonder. Their day started early with mass, then breakfast followed by prayer and off they went to the various places. To the dispensaries in the slums, to the home specially made by Mother where the destitute were treated and kept, to the lepers who needed their attention, always smiling and doing their work with great joy.

Shishu Bhavan became a centre for my awakening, and it was for a number of years that I took myself there with the hope of learning more about Mother. I did not ask questions any more, I just saw and got my answers.

I found out, in the process of growing up, the various meanings of the word vocation. Our Church activities lead us to see the seven sacraments in its true form in close proximity of our everyday life. Baptism, Confirmation, Holy Communion, Penance, Marriage, Anointing of the Sick and The Holy Order. And, as it is known, after birth every child born in a Catholic family receives the first four sacraments at an early age. The other three are for later years of life.

The sacrament that I found that gave a fuller meaning to vocation was the Sacrament of Penance. This sacrament forgives our sins committed after baptism and reconciles us with God if we have separated ourselves from His love. By sin, man separates away from God and by penance he returns to receive His forgiveness. The importance of penance is that upon returning to God with repentance, we change our attitude and decision, from sins, which divides us from His grace. Penance itself has taken various forms of appearance—grief expressed in rending of one's clothes, fasting, sackcloth and ashes, self-infliction and particularly distancing from public life.

However, the essence of penance and the healing of the interior of the self is the cleansing of oneself which is worthy of the act, a change in not only one's external behaviour, but also one's whole life. The change that reaches out from the roots of one's being, right from the new heart placed there by God. Sin and its acts enslave man in such a way that he is incapable of liberating himself, but God in his mercy draws man from his sins back into the communion of life. The advancement for repentance is initiated by God, and the joy caused by the returning sinner reverberates in heaven, for Christ continues His forgiving presence in the community through the sacrament of penance, the open door left to the repentant sinner through which he can return to the communion of life in Christ.

Things began to fall in place; I found that my questions were answered, that my jigsaw puzzle was nearly being completed, and I could distinguish the picture it formed, when I met Dhukhi Ram.

Dhukhi had a vocation too, his vocation came out of the deep love that he felt for Mother, and slowly when we became friends he told me his life's story.

He did not want to commit suicide, but his situation was one of total helplessness and with his meagre income he was at a loss to provide his family with the basics. Dhukhi had no other option but to commit what he did. Upon his being saved, he repented his act of cowardice and with a new life sought God's divine mercy. It wasn't easy; there was this constant nagging thought that all that has happened at this place, being looked after by these sari-clad women was a dream, and that his half-right leg was yet another curse in his life. His illiterate mind gave him little solace and he was often in fits of incoherent banter and the cries of a lost man. The Sisters were always trying to console his wounds and feed him back to life, but his self-torture continued. Till one day, he was taken outdoors for some fresh air.

The balcony kept him away from the sun and he could smell and feel the warm heat of the day with birds chirping somewhere in the trees beyond, and what he heard was something that he never heard before. It was the mid-day adoration when all the Sisters gathered at the small chapel were saying their prayers and singing the Litany of the Saints. The beautiful chorus broke the stillness of the afternoon and it was as if angels had surrounded Dhukhi and were singing to him. He did not know from where the voices came from, till he dragged himself in search for the source, where he found these women in white and blue-bordered saris kneeling in front of a statue of someone with candles burning all around and singing the same music that he heard a little while ago. He was stunned by this vision, for he had never seen anything like this before. He pulled himself up the steps to come closer to where the Sisters were and came to the entrance and felt something happening to him. It was an experience that changed him.

The Sisters departed after their prayers but Dhukhi remained where he was. Each Sister, on passing by him had a smile on her face for him, some even a kind word, which he could not understand. Dhukhi knew that the time had come to do his penance. He stayed there for a long time and it was only when it became dark that he slowly dragged himself to his bed. From that day, he stopped his moaning and groaning and he was always seen at the chapel door, mumbling something to himself.

Many months went by and one day, he called out to one of the Sisters in his Bhojpuri Hindi dialect and enquired who the person was around whom so many candles were burning. But the Sister, not knowing his language only smiled, pointing to the sky above. A gesture of the hand convinced Dhukhi that the person standing there was someone very important, maybe, someone from the heaven.

Dhukhi's penance took shape in the form of two wooden hand grippers. Something in the shape of dumbbells, to carry him to and fro more easily rather than dragging himself to the chapel door. He constructed them all by himself, with the tools provided by the Sisters. A new man was slowly emerging out of the old one and his penance did not cease. He started gathering flowers from the garden and brought them to the chapel door. Cleaned the verandah with a piece of cloth and started talking more frequently with the Sisters, always asking about the statue and the frail lady with lines all over her face. Language was no bar between Dhukhi and the Sisters and both came to know what each other was saying. Dhukhi came to know who the person was in the form of a statue and where to find the lady with lines all over her face.

Dhukhi went to find them both.

Mother was slowly but surely laying down the foundation of her mission. Her call saw her leaving the enclosures of Loreto House, and her seeking permission to start living near the poor and the needy was dispatched to Rome. On granting her request that she could do so, she moved herself to a small tenement close to our house at Creek Lane.

A white sari with blue borders replaced the Loreto habit. A blouse with long sleeves and walking sandals. A blue bag with wooden handles, the ever present rosary tucked at the left side in her waist and the Cross pinned on to the sari on her left shoulder—this was the image that she carried in starting her service to the poor.

Agnes was the youngest child of Nikola and Drana Bojaxhui. They lived in a small Serbian town called Skopje, though they were Albanian. Agnes was fondly called 'Gonxha' in their native language which meant 'Flower Bud'', because she was very pink and plump. During the time of her birth there was a lot of unrest in the Balkans, which resulted to World War I. When Agnes was only eight years old her father died and the family was left grief-stricken. Then again, her brother left home to join the military academy. Agnes was alone with her mother and her sister.

It was during this time that Agnes expressed her desire to become a nun. Her mother played a very important role in her spiritual call, and Agnes with her mother and sister used to go regularly to the shrine of Our Lady of Cernagore in Letnice, in the mountains of Montenegro. It took Agnes many years to try and understand her wish to become a nun and her dream of coming to India. When finally the day came, she told her mother that her heart was set to serve God.

It was a long journey from Skopje to Ireland, but she made it with her friend who was also joining the Loreto noviciate. She settled down and spent the next few weeks learning the English language and coming to know the path that she had chosen. On the Feast of Epiphany, Agnes came to Calcutta and went to the Loreto noviciate in Darjeeling. Agnes took her vows after nearly three years in India, and chose to be named after her patron saint, Saint Therese of Lisieux or Saint Therese of the Child Jesus. But Agnes had a problem as another novice in the same convent had already taken the name of this missionary saint. Agnes dropped the 'h' and the 'e' , added an 'a' and adopted the Spanish version of the same name.

Agnes became Teresa.

From Darjeeling she came to Calcutta. She learned Bengali and Hindi and visited the local parish church, St Teresa of Avila opposite Entally market. It was here that she saw the helplessness and poverty etched all over the nearby streets and for Agnes it was a shock, for she had never seen poverty before. And, Agnes received her second call.

From then on, Sister Teresa tirelessly continued her search for the poor of Calcutta. And, the new congregation of the Missionaries of Charity was approved and instituted in our city. The year was 1950, the same year that I was born.

Teresa's "poor" were those who did not have enough to eat, whose living conditions were against all norms of the dignity of the human self. Deprived, exposed, tortured mentally, materially, spiritually or socially. And the unwanted and unloved.

There were many like these in Calcutta, and one by one they were brought in to be looked after. A superhuman effort coming from a small frail lady. The amazing beauty of her oneness with Christ was her action in showing that all are equal, and that every human life should be recognized for its dignity, its individuality and its immeasurable significance.

She went everywhere, as if she could smell poverty, look into the labyrinths of layers of suffering, feel the cries of distant ailments from forgotten outcastes, hear the soft cry that dustbins held, touch the spirit to let it soar and let life walk in all its manners of living, with laughter filling the days in the comfort of her homes.

Her love spread far and wide; what was instituted in Calcutta spread throughout India and the world. "Lord, make me a channel of Thy peace" was felt everywhere; it was like a tremor, hitting everyone wave after wave. Some saw and felt the tremor, others chose not to see. Those who saw came, joined the mission of love, wearing that simple white sari.

What Teresa saw whilst passing Dharamtalla Street that fateful day on her way to church, was something that we all love and cherish today. The white sari with blue borders. On crossing the intersection she stopped and turned around to the group of women who were sweeping the street. She enquired as to who they were and was told that they were sweepers of Calcutta Corporation. Agnes immediately came to know how she would be attired in her search for the poor. The sari worn by the 'sweepstresses' of Calcutta.

This simple white sari with blue borders has become the best-known uniform in the world. Because Mother knew the best, she did not have one of those suave, debonair designers to design it for her; it was out of her own design and purpose. To be with them, the poorest of the poor. I wish we all wore this uniform irrespective of our gender, our religion, our colour, and our caste or for that matter our ideology. For, if we truly want to wear it then we should wear it in our hearts, because her ideas about the right to live did not slight her right to give, and we can give so much to so many who have none.

By the time I was fifteen, Shishu Bhavan became my place of learning and I came to know about Mother's work in greater detail. Her travels to faraway places in India and abroad. The Missionaries of Charity homes were mushrooming all over the country and the world, and I was as happy as a fifteen-year-old can be, coming to know that she was travelling all around the globe to set up houses for the poor. She toured the world, and went to places that I had never heard of before, and I used to ask the Sisters and my father where they were. My father bought me the Reader's Digest Great World Atlas, and we used to spend a lot of time seeing the maps and finding out the cities where homes were being set up by Mother.

It was thrilling to come to know where Venezuela was, or for that matter, Tabora, a city in Tanzania. Unheard names became a part of my life, and an ongoing geography lesson. Amman in Jordan, Brouke, an Aborigine settlement in Australia, Melbourne, Colombo in Ceylon, Caracas, London. These places were seen by me everyday in the atlas, and I enquired how she went there; "By aeroplane," I was told.

We, of course, had never had the opportunity to fly in one. We did see a few during our visit to the Dum Dum Airport, as it was something that my parents wanted us to see, when one Christmas, my father told all of us that we would go for a plane ride. I was simply ecstatic, we dressed up in our Sunday best and travelled by bus to the Airport where on purchase of the tickets we were ushered to the aircraft.

The plane was a Dakota, which I learnt, with huge propellers making a lot of noise. The backlash of the engine tousled our hair and clothes alike when we were taken into the craft by means of a ladder with railings with the words 'Indian Airlines' written at the sides. We sat in our seats and had to tie ourselves with a belt, which was very difficult, but one of the lady attendants helped us to it and we were given instructions as to how to manage the flight. A glass of orange juice was provided to sooth our nerves, when the aircraft with a jolt started taxing down the runway.

It took about a minute or so when I realized that we had left the ground and were air-borne. Another few minutes passed by when over the loud speakers I could hear instructions as to what to do for the next twenty minutes or so. Like an expert I undid my seat belt, which, I was not knowing a little while ago, and peered through the window. It was a sight that I have remembered till today.

Our beloved city down below, the river like a silver ribbon reflecting the midday sunlight, whiffs of clouds far below, the land sometimes dark green, sometime brown, and the awe of seeing the Howrah Bridge from such a height. The Race Course was visible as a vast piece of green together with the maidan, the city with its buildings were like dwarfs and before I could make out the other landmarks I found that I had to sit again and tie the belt around my waist. I did it with reluctance, but had to, trying to get in as much as possible through the window, when the craft hit the ground with a thud. I knew that the greatest ride of my life was over. But I did ride an aeroplane just like Mother.

I met Mother during the Christmas celebrations at our Church and also at Shishu Bhavan, and could not resist dashing to her direction, touch her feet, wish her "Happy Christmas Māāther," and in the same breath tell her that I have also been in a plane. Her return wish, I recall had an added ring to it, "And Happy Christmas to you too, you will be in many planes when you grow up."

Many years have passed after that Christmas wish and the excitement of a fifteen-year-old boy, and when I started my career I did have the opportunity to be in many planes as Mother said, and whenever I used to step into an aircraft, her words always came back to me. It was like looking at all the flights that she took to distant lands and places to bring love and care, flights of love by an Angel of Love, clad in the cheapest of cloth, for in a world where life is cheap and humanity disregarded without thought, she found that they were worth an idea and a mission.

Sister Teresa needed all the help to begin her mission of love and two of her former pupils came and joined her: Subashini Das and Magdalena Gomes. Sister Teresa became Mother Teresa, Subashini Das became Sister Agnes and Magdalena Gomes became Sister Gertrude.

Dressed in saris, these three sought out the poorest areas in our city, armed with a smile, a kind word, a prayer on their lips walking the dusty streets of Calcutta, conquering poverty with love.

Dhukhi never rested for a long long time in his search to find out who these two persons were. His emotions showed everywhere in the place where he was staying with the Sisters. The small area of grass and trees became his garden, the chapel his prayer room and his own room where there were others, his nights of meditation. This carried on for a long time, when one day he decided to go out and see what the adjoining places were like. He asked the permission from one of the Sisters and went out that day to the market close by.

Entally market is but a few minutes' walk away from where he was staying and in not seeing a big market before he wandered all around the place trying to see the many things the market had to offer, when he came to the flower range. He liked what he saw. The man attending to the flowers thought him to be a beggar wanting alms when Dhukhi in his chaste Bhojpuri Hindi enquired about the price of the beautiful roses that were kept in an earthen pot. The flower vendor was taken aback by his question, thinking what connection a cripple should have with roses, and was about to shoo him off, when Dhukhi took out a few rupees and asked the flower vendor to give him seven roses. The man gave them to Dhukhi not accepting the money and Dhukhi with the roses on his lap came back with a smile on his face.

It was evening and the chapel was full with the Sisters praying. Dhukhi took his place near the door and after the Sisters departed, he went inside and in front of the statue laid the seven yellow roses.

Dhukhi's existence from then on was to search his soul.

I do not know what Dhukhi was searching for, nor do I know what was going on in his mind, but this much I have come to know that there is something beautiful in all of us that allows us to see in us; the sight of love that radiates from that statue in front of which the seven yellow roses were placed, life's wondrous self, allowing us to search the meaning of existence. For, when we find the source that we are looking for, in truth, we receive it in its true form and it shines with us. The seven yellow roses offered by Dhukhi to God was his penance to redeem himself and find Him, every day of the week, for, on the seventh day he saw another week of his existence. An existence, which he never wanted but came to know that he has seen and felt a beautiful person in God and with Him, another. That in his prayer, his existence changed, from weeks to months, from months to years. So that his search would not end, he placed seven yellow roses every seventh day in front of the beautiful person. Always.

Dhukhi never went to get the roses. It came from the flower vendor every seventh day, from Entally market.

His search did not end and neither did mine.

I tried to understand many things, things that were there for a young man to see and touch and feel. I found out that by doing something beautiful for God you actually do something beautiful to man. For, through God you receive man. I came to know what was the meaning of love. I came to know love itself and it was from this small frail woman, who according to me can be described by only one word. Love.

It took many years of my upbringing to understand the beauty of this word, love, and on coming to know its true meaning I came to know the meaning of it. For if Mother did love, and it was with Christ, and without Him and His acts of love we are nothing. There is no religion in this world that does not preach love, for it is peace. And, in peace you will find the beauty of love.

Just like the seven yellow roses offered by Dhukhi to God, an act of supreme love, out of prayer which came from faith, finally making peace with one's own self. Just like the three wrapped in white saris giving love to the many who never saw it before. Love, a continuous process in motion.

I wish all our business cards spell this message and in terms of introduction we can proudly say:

That the fruit of Silence is Prayer
That the fruit of Prayer is Faith
That the fruit of Faith is Love
& That the fruit of Service is Peace.

My days at Shishu Bhavan brought a lot of meaning to the Faith that I belong to. It gave me a whole new meaning to the word faith. We studied catechism in school and also went for Bible studies in Church, and in these classes, the act of Faith was described in its totality. The faith that I came to know was the tireless work that Mother did. Of picking each and every morsel from the acts of love, becoming a servant towards the love for man. She never faltered, her prayer was unseen but felt. Her humbleness came from the epitome of love, for she never asked how much or how little, nor how much that one should do but how much love one should put in it. Not how much we can give but how much love we can give into it. That according to her was the ultimate victory. To love one another.

Our commitment to our society does not end by giving a few alms to the poor and downtrodden, but to provide love and caring. What I started learning from Mother was exactly that. In serving the needs of the poor the attention is to those who are unwanted and deprived of love. Love, has its many connotations but the supreme act of such love is to make the person feel whole. To be loved, to be cared, to be understood and to be respected as a human being. There have been times when we have failed to show such acts of comforting, but if we just throw away our pride and dwell in one another, in the comfort that each other brings, that will be our love for God and to man.

When the Missionaries of Charity was instituted, my parents told me that the decree of its recognition was read by Mother's spiritual advisor amidst pin-drop silence at our church. Today, that message of love still echoes in the recesses of my mind.

That to fulfil the mission of compassion and love, to the poorest of the poor, we must go to wherever it is possible, seeking out towns and villages all over the world, even amongst squalid surroundings to find the poorest, the abandoned, the sick, the infirm, the leper, the dying, the desperate, the lost, the outcast and take care of them, rendering them help, visiting them tirelessly, living Christ's love for them and awakening their response to His great love.

I have yet to find any mission in this world that speaks such language of love.

I sketched many portraits of Mother, but I am yet to sketch the best of her. And, I do not know whether I will be able to do it, for honestly, I do not have the skill of showing all her qualities on a single canvas, of her visage and her countenance that speaks of love.

Over the years of my going to Shishu Bhavan I found that she not only opened my eyes with her creed of giving, but also taught me the art of living.

The visions of a twelve-year-old will never be erased from the same man who has seen fifty-two summers, for in the autumn of my life when I will reach my destination, I would like to be a part of the last station created by Ma, my Mother, from where I will sit at the right hand of God and Mother in one.

In the early seventies, 1971 to be exact, we all went to the concelebrated mass held at our church, which was for the Award that Mother received from Pope Paul VI. Our church was packed to its capacity and additional chairs and speakers were placed for the many who took their place outdoors. I was then in the church choir and the choir loft was the place where I was, watching the proceedings below.

My friend was the choirmaster and a secular priest who studied church music and I learnt from him some of the beautiful songs composed by the "Sacred Sons," Ave Maria being one of them. It was supposed to be sung after the communion and I sang Franz Schubert's opus No.52 the way he wrote it for "The Maiden." It is a song that I will never forget because the ethos of what Mother was, was there in the words and the tune both in Latin and English; written 100 years before Mother's birth.

"Ave Maria.
Gratia plena
Maria, gratia plena,
Maria, gratia plena.
Ave, ave! dominus,
Dominus tecum.
Benedicta tu in mulieribus,
Et benedictus,
Et benedictus fructus ventris,
Ventris tui, Jesus.
Ave Maria.

Ave Maria.
Mater Dei,
Ora pro nobis pecca to ribus,
Ora, ora pro nobis pecca to ribus
Nunc et in ho ra mortis,
In hora mortis nostrae,
In hora mortis, mortis nostrae,
In hora mortis nostrae.
Ave Maria.

Ave Maria.
Gratia plena,
Maria, gratia plena,
Maria, gratia plena,
Ave, ave! dominus,
Dominus tecum,

Benedicta tu in mulieribus,
Et benedictus,
Et benedictus fructus ventris,
Ventris tui, Jesus.
Ave Maria."

"Ave Maria.
Maiden mild!
Listen to a maiden's pray'r,
For thou canst hear though from the wild,
Thou canst save amid despair, amid despair.
Safe may we sleep beneath Thy care,
Tho' banished, out cast and reviled.
O Maiden hear a maiden's prayer,
O Mother, hear a suppliant child!
Ave Maria.

Ave Maria!
Undefiled!
The flint y couch we now must share,
Shall seem with down of eider piled.
If Thy protection, if Thy protection hover there,
The murky cavern's heavy air,
Shall breathe of balm if Thou hast smiled.
Thou Maiden hear a maiden's prayer,

Mother, hear a suppliant child.
Ave Maria!

Ave Maria!
Stainless styled!
Foul demons of the Earth and Air,
From this their wonted haunt exiled,
Shall flee before Thy presence.
Thy presence fair,
We bow unto our lot of care,
Beneath Thy guidance reconciled.
Hear for a maid, a maiden's prayer,
And for a father hear a child!
Ave Marua!"

The award was instituted by Pope John XXIII for Peace, and this reward befitted the person who brought peace to so many souls in our world.

Dhukhi Ram was clothed, fed, looked after and got a place to stay. His ailments were taken care of and his wounds started to heal. His coughing stopped and he regained his strength. He was slowly becoming normal again. And, he prayed to his god that he should live and be of some use to the cause of this woman who gave him a new life, and in his search he found them both.

One who taught love and gave mankind its meaning, the other that gave love and cared for mankind, with just two thousand years between them.

And, Dhukhi never failed to place the seven yellow roses on the seventh day, to a beautiful person. Always. And neither did I.

Calls are of different kinds, I came to know. The call that came to the young girl named Agnes, and another call to the same person, the manifestation that we see today. The call of repentance that came to an illiterate man from nowhere, who repented and became whole. The call to love, the call to repent all embodied in the act called faith, for without faith you cannot continue in the process of truth, and without truth you cannot love.

After six years, Dhukhi Ram on a wheel-chair became the assistant to the gate-keeper.

And, I came to know that Faith can move mountains.

For, she taught me Faith. And how to love God's children.

An Act of Hope

Faith, which admits one to the unseen realities; and love, which is actually faith in action; comes hope, to sustain the being through the life of pilgrimage. In this pilgrimage of life, one's sufferings become one's pride. For, suffering brings patience, patience brings perseverance and perseverance brings hope. Hope is not deceptive, because the love of God has been poured into our hearts, which prompts us to look to faith for those rewards that righteousness bring. Hope, therefore, is not just natural longing; like faith, but an aspect of the gift of salvation, and through hope grows fulfilment.

Hope, the object of one's expectation is divided by a gulf called fear. And who can assuage this fear? Who can heal the wounds of this fear to the man without hope? The being that needs confidence, comfort, and solace. He is too convinced of his apparent worthlessness, what the being lacks is not knowledge, rather the hope and strength to rise from the filth.

These beings, got hope from a person whom they did not know. They found their strength springing from hope that will conquer their fear.

This was the act of hope given by the lady from Skopje.

HOPE

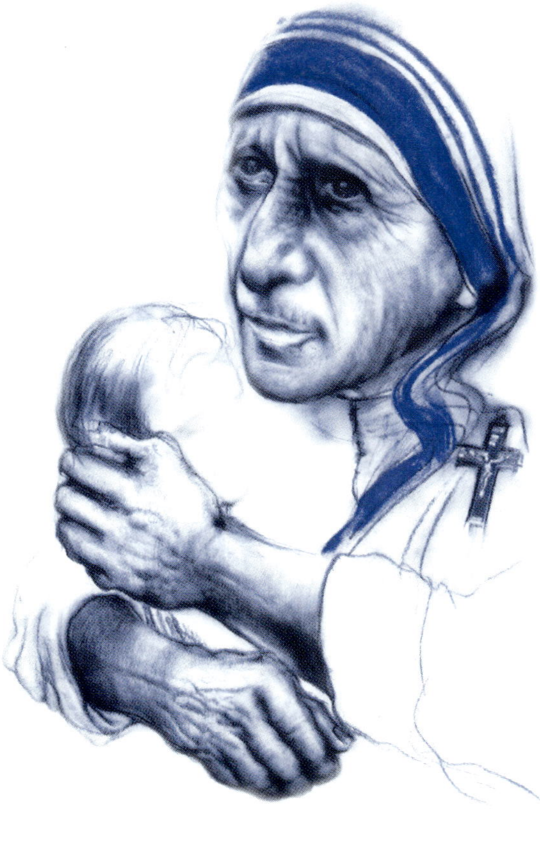

May I bring Hope, Lord, where there are shadows…

Meet Fatima

SHE was an educated woman, having completed her education from the local school, and wished to study further, something unheard of in the small Muslim community of Tiljala, in the outskirts of Calcutta. She also started teaching in the same school, where her teachers were very happy and proud of her. Fatima decided to do something about herself and not be like the many whom she saw daily in her locality and community. In an orthodox community, at least as far as women were concerned, Fatima was a rebel, for it was totally unheard of for a Muslim girl to work and earn her living. Her world consisted of the school and the tailor's shop in front of her bustee. The tailor, elderly and learned, taught her the verses from the Holy Book, which were a delight to her ears.

She had been a very intelligent and curious girl from a young age, and wanted to find out about everything. Her parents, not knowing what to do with the inquisitive child, got her admitted to the local school. Her days were spent with the other students and in the afternoon she came back to learn the holy words of the Quran from the tailor in front of her home. She came to know the five continents, the seasons and the leap year. As letters of the alphabet turned into words, she learnt to spell her name with her slate and chalk. She wrote her sister's and brother's names too.

And, they were all in English. Her learning of the Holy Book began at an early age with the tailor; under the street lamps she learnt the beautiful words of wisdom and felt the truth of submission. Fatima was learning that life was made out of love, of humanness, of sorrow and of repentance. She had questions for the tailor all the time and he answered from the Holy Book.

As Fatima grew from a child to a young woman, her quest for knowledge brought her closer to total ännihilation, for everybody in her locality thought that she had come to know more than anybody else. Her school going and teaching the children stopped, her meeting the old tailor was never again to be as he was packed off with his belongings to another place by the local people, and Fatima became a chained woman in her own house, when her parents decided to get her married.

Being born as a girl seemed to be the greatest curse in her life. She was the ninth in a long line of nine other sisters and three brothers. A thorn in the already burdened family of Mir Quasim Hyder Ali.

Exactly four days after her wedding to a local butcher, her nightmare began. Fatima's four days of wedded bliss were shattered when she stepped out of her in-laws' house in search of the old tailor in order to learn more from the Holy Book. She was abused and accused by her in-laws, insulted by her husband and her own parents, of committing a forbidden act. She was locked up in her room for days on end, with insults heaped upon her, when finally she could not take it anymore; she decided to take her own life.

She took her life, dousing herself with kerosene and setting herself ablaze, a human torch that could not take the pain anymore, when her cries were heard by the neighbours in the middle of the afternoon. Fatima was half-gone when the door was broken down, and the flame doused by pieces of cloth and water. Her body lay charred on the floor, stinking of burnt flesh, burnt hair and kerosene. She did not die, but suffered third degree burns.

She was rushed by neighbours to a nearby clinic where after first aid she was taken to the government hospital. The doctors and nurses at the emergency ward found that her burns had taken a serious turn, and she was laid on a metal stretcher with a blanket covering her body. But the hospital refused to take her in saying that self-immolation was a police case, and that they should find some other cause for her burns. Meanwhile, her family, her husband or his family had not come either as they were the least interested anyway.

So, Fatima was outside the hospital building, fighting for her life, when three Missionaries of Charity Sisters saw the grey blanket half covering a partly bandaged charred body. Ebbing away from the life that she so strongly wanted, Fatima did not know what was happening around her. Her conscious self or whatever that was left of it, was in too much pain. Her mind spiralled towards and away from consciousness. She was sliding and slipping fast into the darkness away from the unbearable pain. She dreamt of the holy words that had been taught to her, and started reciting them even as she fell into the depths of the black unknown.

When, opening her eyes oneday, she saw this smiling face with lines all over her face cradling her head in her lap.

There was hope after all.

Getting down to Business

Teresa knew that she had to get some funds to start her school in the slums. She went to some of the fathers at St Teresa's, Entally, who gave her few rupees from their pocket money and her first slum school was set up.

Forty years ago, I did not understand "Yet not I, but Christ liveth in me," a favourite saying of Mother's at all. But in trying to decipher its meaning, I assumed the tacit, unspoken word of the living, and took her commandment in great seriousness. Was it understood by all? In my case, I learned, though it took me a long, long time.

I learned how this woman had left everything to Him, because He did live in her. This belief is not acquired, nor taught, nor picked up from any departmental store. It is inborn. And, she worked towards the journey of her inner self towards Him. It was hard work, indeed.

Accommodation for the Sisters, food, clothing, kitchen utensils, accommodating the destitute, the children, the lepers, the dying … the list is endless. How did she do it? From where did she get the money? Who were the benefactors?

Since I stopped asking questions, I ventured out to find out by myself, and again it revealed how sincere and honest was her one-with-God attitude, that she knew that He would take care of all the needs. Mother needed money, and it came to her in the most uncommon circumstances.

It was 1964. My parents had gone to Bombay on the occasion of the visit of Pope Paul VI. On their return, many days followed in hearing the stories of the wonderful time that they had at Bombay, a place none of us including my parents had been to. They brought together with them many artefacts of the Pontifical visit, comprising various medallions, postcards, a memento of the altar where the Holy Father celebrated mass and black and white photographs of their sojourn in Bombay city. But when we were told that His Holiness had left his car behind for Mother, I got excited. My father explained that the car would soon be in Calcutta and we could all go and have a look because he had seen nothing like that before.

Neither had I, for that matter, and the car was something out of this world. It was a sleek, white limousine so long and big that it was on permanent show at our Church compound, too big for any one of Mother's home to garage. I came to know that it was called a Lincoln Continental.

One evening, my father came home from work to let us know that maybe, one day we could even ride the car as it could become ours. It was a bombshell. I shot question after perplexed question as to what was his reason for hoping for such an absurd dream. Then I came to know that Mother had turned this gift to her into a raffle. Soon, everybody had bought the raffle tickets in the hope that they would drive this beautiful white car someday. I lovingly saw it everyday, always wondering where my father will park it if he won.

He did not win the raffle, but Mother raised enough money for her future home for the lepers.

This was one of the ways that God provided her with money. "Leave it unto Him," and the money came, from various sources. From the well-endowed, who never felt the pinch and gave it for her cause. From the people of our locality, in whatever small way they could afford. From the benefactors from overseas, where her cause was well known. From individuals, from their monthly salaries. It all came, slowly and steadily allowing Mother to build her mission of love.

Our family had its small share of giving to Mother's cause. My mother was an excellent knitter and a seamstress. We had a hand-operated sewing machine and my mother started sewing the blue bags that are now practically as famous as the sari itself. I was then studying at Don Bosco and the curriculum also had vocational training, woodwork being one of them. I used to buy the plywood, my father made the template for the handles, and I had the handles crafted out with my fret saw, sandpapering them and polishing them for my mother to do the final stitching. Come winter, and winter used to set early then in Calcutta, my mother would start knitting the pullovers for the Sisters to wear during the colder months. It may not have been much, but that was what we could afford from my father's income.

I met Fatima actually by chance. A friend wished to feed the poor on her father's death anniversary. I was asked what would be the best possible way to do it, when I recollected that the food supplied to the Home for Dying Destitute, set up by Mother, were sometime given by such persons in their act of charity and for their departed beloved. We immediately went to Nirmal Hriday and there I met Fatima.

Nirmal Hriday is a home for the dying destitute, adjacent to the famous Kali temple in Calcutta. It is a long room with arched windows, half-way up in the walls, whilst the remaining half has concrete about two and a half feet in height against both the walls with a depth of about six feet. A similar concrete structure is in the middle with a passage way all around it. The concrete supports rows of mattresses upon spring stretchers with their occupants. I must confess that it was not a very pleasant sight to behold.

As a Calcuttan, I must admit that I have seen such emaciated creatures on and off around the city, but the sight of their grief caught me unawares. I had to control myself at this stomach-churning scene and left the room to light a cigarette outside, trying my best to rest my heaving stomach, when I remembered Milton's words of sadness and my own self-remorse:

"That I witnessed huge affliction and dismay,
Mixed with obdurate pride and steadfast hate.
At once, as far as angels can see, he views
The dismal situation waste and wild:
A dungeon horrible, on all sides round
As one great furnace flamed..."

The physical look of that place had repelled me, but when I saw many groups from around the world walk in, touch the statue beside the door, cross themselves with the holy water, wear the surgical gloves and help the Sisters, I began to cry. I was ashamed that I, a part of these very souls living in my city did not have the courage to see the reality of life. That these dying are one of us and that one person thought about them. What I witnessed was human degradation at its lowest level, but, the cleanliness, the calmness, the tranquillity of the place hit my emotions. Reading and reciting Milton in Class Eight was not understood in its true form, which after twenty-seven years, took but just a moment. And, I came to know the meaning of "Yet not I, but Christ liveth in me."

It became a regular routine of sorts sometime in the evenings and sometime in the mornings whenever my free time allowed me, sometime two, three times a week, sometime even after weeks, but I made an effort to go to Nirmal Hriday, the place for the dying. And, how aptly the name was given to this place, which was the last station between life on earth and eternal life.

Clean Heart. For in Bengali, "Nirmal" means "Clean" and "Hriday" means "Heart". A place that is difficult to find in normal circumstances, but a place that was created out of a clean heart. For, the cleansing was in both ways, for the inmates as well as the outsiders like me. Of a resurrection in life and of a resurrection thereafter.

In one of my visits I saw this rather crumpled figure on the same mattress like others in an adjacent room next to the main hall. One of the sisters was feeding this figure and another was attending to its wounds. The figure was completely bound with bandage and a small opening where her mouth was, was all that could be seen. On enquiring I was told how this girl got burnt and was brought to Nirmal Hriday.

Fatima was declared clinically dead. But she got the same treatment like the others or maybe, a bit more by the visiting Sisters from Rome. One of whom was a final year medical student. The treatment was with the help of the local doctor who was always in attendance day and night, her wounds cleansed and new gauge and bandages were wrapped around. This carried on for months and whenever I went over I always stood by helplessly seeing this extreme act of cleansing take place patiently. The condition of this girl was known to many as it was reported in the dailies and one day after nearly two years, in one of my visits I found a crowd gathered in front of the door. On entering with difficulty I found that there were many Sisters around where Fatima lay. My heart skipped a beat and one of the Sisters coming to know me exclaimed. "Fatima spoke today, she said, Abba."

Miracles did happen in the twentieth century, I thought. Miracles of the human kind, where life is restored again by love and care. Day after day, month after month of never tiring selves dedicated to the one cause of redemption. Their sufferings were the Sisters suffering too. As Christ wanted to help in sharing with our life, our loneliness, our agony and our death so did they, these white sari-clad Angels of Love. Their belief that being one with the sufferers they can redeem them, for by bringing God into their lives they were bringing them to God.

The Loreto habit having been discarded saw a new person emerging. Her vision shifted towards the poorest of the poor.

To look after them better she undertook a crash course at Patna for three months. Learning to nurse people back to life again.

Mother was born on 26 August 1910 and by the time she was thirty-eight in the year 1948, she established the beginning of her mission. It was a slum school. Her mission expanded and the Missionaries of Charity was formed. Shishu Bhavan was opened. Nirmal Kennedy Center near the airport took shape. Nirmal Hriday, the House for the Dying Destitutes was opened together with the Calcutta Corporation. A home for lepers at Shanti Nagar. Noviciates, homes for the Sisters. Home for some more lepers around the country. Homes for the Dying Destitutes around the country and the world.

I was baffled. How could this lady do all this? Even some of the best-known corporate houses would be shamed at the way her empire of love was increasing. No advertising campaign, no catchy slogans, no fund-raising dinner parties. None at all. But it happened.

It happened with a passion called LOVE. Love the greatest provider of all.

John Donne, one of the great poets of the early seventeenth century wrote a very soul-stirring peom named, *Hymn to God, My God*. One stanza expresses the line above:

"We think that Paradise and Calvary,
Christ's Cross and Adam's tree, stood in one place;
Look, Lord and find both Adams met in me;
As the first Adam's sweat surrounds my face,
May the last Adam's blood my soul embrace."

How true! How true are the words of John Donne. For, if it wouldn't have been for both, Adam and Him, where would we embrace ourselves in love? It was the sweat, it was the blood, and it was the dying soul in creation that we find our place of loving. Never to leave both, in Paradise or at Calvary.

This super-abundance of God in Christ comes out very strongly, where the beginning of man together with the death of man is His blessing. In the fullness of time, comes to us that search and embraces our soul with love. Love is not a one-way traffic, it is an all-embracing relation between people. And, with this love comes hope, which provides.

Mother was provided with the abundance that few giants in the corporate world can muster. Her strategy, a mind-boggling theme for copywriters. Her media exercise, a mix of subdued penetration and gentle aggressiveness. Her tools, a white sari and words of love on her lips. Her communication plan, recite the rosary all the time, whenever you are free. Her signature, "Love thy neighbour."

No TV blitzkrieg, no full page colour ads, no radio jingles, no outdoor campaigns. Just three little words. "LOVE THY NEIGHBOUR."

In getting down to business, Mother was possibly the greatest strategist in the modern times, and most who know about her will surely agree. Her shrewdness in achieving the one and only thing from humans for humans was legendary. Her goal set, never wavered, and more than once she came out as the winner. She new what she was up against, and she smites across any obstacles with these three little words.

Her love gave hope to millions across the world. This small frail sari-clad lady called, Hope.

Many years passed and one day I decided to go and visit Nirmal Hriday. I enquired about the girl named Fatima to one of the Sisters. She was a little surprised as to my asking this particular question, and not seeing me before, replied that Fatima has left and is currently teaching in a school. My reaction must have shown on my face for the Sister enquired whether something was wrong with me. I replied her in the negative and left.

That evening, listening to Dvorak's "New World" Symphony, I saw Fatima, and many other Fatimas like her, clinging to that last spark called hope. Laying their heads on a lap called hope. Living again a life of the living given by a soul who loved them, and who gave them hope. Hope, the reward of ease, safety and security. A new world to live in, a *"Natun Jibon"*[1] all over again.

And I came to know that Hope can bring salvation.

Religious instructions are of the mental kind. They give you a warmth of stability, wrapping your senses with cotton and wool, allowing the memory to nourish in the newfound wisdom, like the Garden of Eden. Of understanding the ethos of the fundamental beginnings of life and the value that it deserves. Our religious classes attended by our respective age groups saw and delved into the background of the promise and fulfilment of hope. It did not come easily. It was difficult at that point in time. But the windows of the mind opened, and gradually the structure of hope materialized.

1 Natun Jibon in Bengali means — New Life.

Hope as perceived, brought redemption of the world, once and for all. And, through baptism you become a sharer in that redemption. For, without baptism, you cannot be pure. As purification is a prescribed act of washing. Of moral goodness. Through the waters of baptism and with the words of invocation a person comes in contact with the visible humanity of the saving act. What happens in baptism is that the sin-bound person over whom the water is poured is immersed in redemption and comes from the alive with a new life. He does not live to himself but to God. The redemptive spirit poured abundantly into the hearts of the baptised entitles them to cry out "Abba, Father" allowing them the full privilege of son-ship. Hope justifies this privilege and one becomes coheirer to the kingdom of God.

Our religious instructions taught us to see through hope, but the realities into which we were introduced taught us to see with the eyes of faith. With water and the word, active and alive in the work of the community. I started to learn the meaning of hope through what Mother taught, that if you enfold yourself with His love, then it is assured that nothing can snatch one away from His grace. The reality, however, is that you must work towards it.

Fatima believed in hope and saw it through the eyes of faith and she resurrected to a new life. Fatima, the Queen of the Heavens believed in Hope and its provider.

Fatima's wounds healed, but her entire body, head downwards, was pockmarked, and the skin discolouration was very apparent with no hair on her head. Her eyes had a distant look and her lips were constantly parted showing her somewhat even teeth with a smile to it. Her right hand was slightly bent and her left leg was still a bit painful. She wore new sandals and walked every morning from her foster-parent's home to Rafi Ahmed Kidwai Road, eight o'clock sharp for the assembly and start her day in school.

I saw Fatima from a distance, when I came to know where she was teaching and the many years of her struggle with life came back to me and I had to control myself. What I saw was a new person, in a bright flowery printed sari, carrying an ordinary cloth bag, perhaps with her midday tiffin and her class books, walking with a slight limp, but with her head held high. A new and resurrected person in her own life, limping towards her goal. And, I was sure, Fatima had the prayer on her lips that she came to know and understand from the many white sari-clad women with blue borders who looked after her. That the value of a soul was placed in the hands by God, that God wanted something to be done for her, that we are all bound by the conscience of salvation. The ever-lasting covenant of our souls through hope.

For, isn't Paradise and Calvary side by side, allowing us to work towards Him, moving Him towards us, towards the fruits of redemption in one's own resurrection.

Fatima became the Assistant Principal of the school after seven years.

And, I came to know that hope is an expectation redeemed by mankind.

An Act of Charity

Who creates such works of Charity? Thyself, or others. Or, that defying soul that does not want to see purgatory.

Charity transcends all other human endeavour. And this, all embracing relationship between people reaching from the depths of the psyche includes loyalty, dedication, knowledge to understand, mutuality, responsiveness, and responsibility, and of course "Love" that alludes all. Man's reception of these gifts matured into love. And, Charity is Love.

And God is Love. God's love is made evident to man in the flesh of his Son, whom He sent into this world, that we might have life through Him. The proof that this life is in us consists in the love that we manifest to one another.

No one has ever seen God. Yet, if we love one another, God dwells in us and his love is brought to perfection in ourselves. Christ, the evidence of God's love for us, lives on, in us through the Holy Spirit that is given to us in accordance with Christ's own promise.

That the way we know we remain in Him and He in us, that He has given us of His Spirit.

If God is love, the Christian reality is a share in that love, through which the Spirit transmits to us Christ's life, by which we become God's children.

For Mother the relationship between God and man was paramount. For, in the power of God's saving love, man fulfils the prophecy of evangelising the poor, to heal the contrite of heart, to liberate the captives, to bring sight to the blind and healing to those who are broken and downhearted. And when her "Love Incorporated" was established, the blind recovered their sight, the cripples walked, the lepers were cured, the deaf could hear and the poor knew that they could get something to eat.

These were her Acts of Charity, to cement the communion that is also the consummation.

CHARITY

Make us worthy, Lord, to serve our fellowmen...

Meet Mary Bella

DURING the time of partition, when India gained Independence, another country was born; East Bengal, as it was known during the British period, became East Pakistan. Thousands left their homeland to set up home again next door. Mary and her family were one of them. Mary was two-and-a-half years old when she and her parents and two brothers walked, travelled in a bullock-cart, crossed the mighty Meghna in a country boat, walked again, finally arriving at a place where there were thousands waiting to cross over to an unknown land and country. They were the refugees of Independence.

Mary Bella Mondal, a baptised Christian from Borisal, had her name entered in the Government of India register of emigration, as were her two older brothers and her parents. Oblivious of the crowd and the jostling, Mary slept comfortably in her mother's lap. The Mondal family from Borisal crossed the new border and unbeknownst to them, entered a nightmare that would plague them throughout their life. Mary Bella became a victim of a new, unknown destiny. Her parents contacted the dreaded disease known as leprosy.

It happened as they were trying to settle down in the border towns of West Bengal. They migrated constantly from village to village, seeking employment, finally making a structure of bamboo and mud with a roof of borrowed, broken terracotta tiles tied together with jute twine—home at last in a growing village called Bishtupur.

Her childhood was like a weathervane braving a storm. It deepened, the vortex directly on that small hut of the Mondal family. Soon, they were outcastes. The brothers and sister found some forgotten strips of wood and made a trolley for their parents to walk.

They took it by turns, the older of them in the morning, the middle one in the afternoon and the youngest in the evening. The plan suited them well. The elder after his bout could cook for the others, the middle one after his time could tend to their housekeeping, and as for Mary Bella, she only had to cover her parents with a sheet at night. This was the daily routine, now that they had to beg for food. Meanwhile, part by part of their decrepit structure vanished, and one day the structure of bamboo, mud and broken terracotta tiles disappeared completely. How? Mary Bella did not know, but disappear it did. From then on, they were at the fringes of the railway station, when one day when she was fifteen they boarded a train, not knowing its destination, and they found themselves in a place called Sealdah.

By that time, her father's hands had disfigured from wrist downwards. Her mother's head was a bald pate of festered skin. Her toes looked as if her foot had swallowed them. Her eyes did not have their lashes. Her brothers were not as spirited as before. She laid down beside her parents and brothers on platform number

6 at Sealdah Station, wondering what befell them. When the ordeal started.

Mary Bella was half-way between the beautiful feeling of awakenss and deep slumber, when, she felt herself being poked with sticks. She awoke and registered herself to this intrusion and found to her disbelief a gang of young men passing lured remarks to her. Her mind in turmoil she brushed aside these insults and dragged herself up, to find shelter with her brothers and her parents. To her disbelief she found that she was all alone. Mary Bella Mondal, fifteen years old fell into the clutches of the hungry animals called human beings.

She was found far away from the platform the next day in a dazed stupor by the track cleaning squad, bleeding and bruised all over, two teeth missing, and with blood dripping down her. Mary Bella was helped by a woman from the cleaning squad to the Station Master's office. She lay on the floor covered by a green sheet of the Indian Railways, wondering where her family was. Did they face the same fate or were they taken away somewhere. Her mind was a whirlpool of questions and finding no answers, she began to cry asking for death to come by.

By the time the Station Master arrived, Mary Bella had slipped into unconsciousness, and was handed over to the police in that state. The police, not knowing what to do with her, sent her to a juvenile home where the torture began.

It was the cold sting of a pail of water that woke her up. She was heckled, jostled, abused and she was hit by women—some older than her and some younger. Some dragged her by her hair, whilst some mocked her on seeing her front two teeth missing. This carried on day after day, week after week, when one day a burly matronly woman commanded her to accompany her to her quarters. She gave Mary Bella some food, a frock to wear, some little money and instructed her to leave the premises at nightfall: "Go to Entally, to Shishu Bhavan."

Not familiar with the city, Mary Bella walked the major part of the evening enquiring all the time as to where Shishu Bhavan was. Tired, exhausted, drained out and helpless, she sat on the kerb of the pavement at the crossing of a busy intersection and fell asleep.

The clash of cymbals and drums woke her up the next morning. The group comprised two men and three women, with one on a wooden trolley and one pulling, while the rest beating the rhythm. They took her into their fold. Mary Bella thought that at last, she had found some decent people who were friendly enough to accept her, and she recognized them. The banner held by the man who played the drum looked very familiar to Mary Bella and said it all, "Help the Lepers."

Love Incorporated

Mother's unconditional love through Faith, Hope and Charity saw innumerable houses built for the poor around the world, where love abides, and love is shared by the countless persons who have forsaken the worldly life to be one with Mother's call of loving and serving the poor.

It was sometime during the mid-1990s, that a musical programme was held at the beautiful lawns of St Paul's Cathedral, Calcutta. On the opening evening, Mother was invited to inaugurate the event, and though unwell, she came. I was privileged to conduct the programme and had the honour of requesting her to light the lamp and declaring the three-day programme officially open. Mother said to the two thousand-strong audience on that November evening: "Love God and love your neighbour, for to love God and to love your neighbour is inseparable. For if we do not love God we cannot love our neighbour."

The applause was deafening, whilst the television cameras rolled. This was how strong her conviction was of her message, and the almost magical way she pulls all who sees, hear and feel her. I felt blessed to be standing beside her, holding the same candle with which she lit the lamp.

Mother's love was for all. Love is an all-embracing relationship between people, that reaches from the depths of their psyche and includes loyalty, dedicatedness, intimate knowledge, mutuality, responsiveness and responsibility and of course, love for God. The love of God for man is manifested in creation and above all in election. To have been chosen to carry out God's commandments. All that was involved in God's creation, and election, and man's reception of these gifts matured into love.

And, Mother's commandment was very simple. If you do not love mankind that was created by God, how can you love Him in return? You had to love both in equal terms, as the great commandment says: "You shall love the Lord, your God with all your heart, and with all your soul, and with all your strength." An extremely basic, simple statement to live with. But it had to take a person like Mother to literally open the eyes of the world for them to feel and hear the cries of the neighbour next door. Or, did they?

Her 'Love Incorporated' brought together people in thousands, and they came from all walks of life, young and middle-aged and old, from around the world. From Kerala, from Orissa, from Bengal, from Karnataka, from Gujarat. From Arkansans, from Florence, Italy, from Andalusia, from Alaska, from the farthest Hebrides; they all came, for the call was as clear as a trumpet to where they belonged. A not-too-difficult proposition, for they all had something to tell in their own little way that they also loved and would dedicate their life for caring of the poor. They all came to be a part of this phenomenon called 'Love Incorporated' as I found the Missionaries of Charity to be.

Where will you ever see such determination of faith? A countenance so small encased a heart so big for the world, because when you say "Mother" people never ask who you are referring to. Because a Nobel for Peace brought great honour to our country, who made this city and country her home. Because she became a mirror for our souls, and the legacy that she left behind will uphold her cause that is Love Incorporated.

Mother's credo was to unite each other in prayer and sacrifice. Not a difficult task, as we all pray for something or the other. We all make sacrifices for our family, our parents, our children, our near and dearest one, don't we? So, why not unite in prayer and sacrifice for the downtrodden and the poorest of the poor? Her love towards these poor was her way of telling us to be of assistance in recognizing God in the person of the poor. In recognizing God's love better through the works of Charity and of service to the poor. Of lending a hand to her cause, so that the world becomes a better place to live in. So that all of us become her co-workers, in the true spirit of togetherness.

The past reveals the great creative force of individual human beings, who through their single thought of determination, achieved so much despite human weakness and imperfections. It demonstrates again and again that faith, an indestructible vitality, can face many challenges at even the most difficult times. The mind of an Albanian emigrant, through prayer, conquered the most difficult of situations. The language was of no consequence to her, as she knew there was no language to describe love or to show it, but only by giving. Her physical attributes did not hinder the powerful opponents that she met, and the insuperable obstacles that she faced. Her colour or her looks did not matter to her either, for she knew where she was headed. To create a bond between man and man, to live in harmony and care for each other.

I must live alone outside, I must leave the cloister and be closer to the poor, in the slums.

If this was the thought that was going on in the mind of the thirty-six-year old Agnes, then I must say, God revealed again to us the sacrifices undertaken by the Israelites in their long journey to freedom. Mother embarked on her second journey to free the poor from the shackles of depravity, just like the Israelites, and gave them their freedom. In the love between God and man, what is paramount is the initiative on the part of God, for God sent his Son as an offering. The initiative is evident enough that the Son of

Man came to search out and save what was lost. Mother came from a distant land, stayed back, and searched to save what was lost. A truly difficult task in a foreign land, with an alien tongue and an alien climate.

She did not mind leaving her comfortable home in the sleepy village of Skopje, the comfort of the warm fireplace in the evenings and the affectionate embrace of her parents. But she wanted to leave and come to India. She could have gone somewhere else, but God's call manifests itself in such wonders. We received her, she was sent to us, to this city of Calcutta, as an offering for our sins. And, she fulfilled the prophecy, so that the blind could see, the cripples could walk again, that the lepers could live a meaningful life, the deaf could hear the astonishing wonder of creation, the dead are revived to live again with hope, and that the poor have the good news of their salvation.

Any suffering has a reward, for suffering itself is nothing till the suffering is shared with Adam and Him, both in Paradise and Calvary. For, this is a wonderful gift received by man, for at death we will not be judged by the amount of work we did but the love we have put into it. And, this love is self-sacrifice, of the giving and the feeling. Till it hurts.

From olden times as written in the Holy Scriptures, leprosy was a scourge to the victim as well as the society where he lived. It was a wound for banishment. From your own family and from the people around you. In such sorrow, these men and women of God lived a life of begging and ostracism.

I am sure no human being could possibly dream that something like this could happen to him. But then it did, to the many who contracted this disease. For these classic outcastes from humanity, from whom we shrink and run away. But Mother's unfathomable love towards these children brought them from the brink of isolation as outcastes of humanity and placed them in Shanti Nagar, the Town of Peace, shunned no more from the very world they lived in, but in peace and harmony amongst themselves created by Mother.

Our country has its share of lepers, from the upper echelons to the depths of poverty where such souls live with the trepidation of being a great evil to society. But the malaise is not as despicable as to be denied love and be abandoned.

During the early 1970s, certain things happened in my life that have stayed with me forever. One such was the death of my father, which proved extremely traumatic for me in the threshold of my adolescence. Shishu Bhavan, as always, became a balm to my raw nerves during those days and so was my Church. It took sometime for the rawness to heal, but the residual effect remains till today. What allowed me to set forth my direction of healing was what I saw after coming out from Church, one day after the evening mass. It was the sound of a rhythm of wanting.

I had never seen lepers before. And, this rhythm took me towards where they were standing. Right in front of Entally market I saw this group of about six to eight somewhat cheerful people with bandaged hands and legs. Two of them were on wheelbarrow-like objects and the others were beating the rhythm that drew me towards them. One had a kettledrum, which made a sharp distinct beat, the others had metal maracas, and cymbals, and one had a flute. This sight, like something I had never seen before made me enquire as to who they were, and prompt came the reply from an elderly bystander: "Lepers".

I must confess it was not the best of sights to behold. They carried on their rhythm and some, in between the beat put forth an aluminum cup, which contained some money and jingled them to keep with the beat of the rhythm. I managed to take out some coins and drop them in the aluminum cup and to my amazement I found that I recognized their rhythm and the beat. It was the young girl who was playing the flute, though not very professionally, but the tune was recognizable. She was a bit older than me I thought, but her appearance did not suggest any of the aliments the others bore. Her face was well scrubbed, hair tied in a tight bun, her clothes clean and above all, what caught my attention was her fingers; long and graceful, trapping and releasing the notes from her flute. It was the opening bars of "We shall overcome."

This young girl came forward blowing into her flute, wrapping the notes made famous by Pete Seger whilst the others carried on playing their own instruments. I could not help but to hum with her the stanzas that I knew by heart, and she opened her eyes, stopped playing and smiled. I found that two of her front teeth were missing.

I must do something for them. They are God's children and they are mine, too.

Mother's love poured out on these victims of leprosy, young and old alike, some of them unable to walk, just crawl. She, indeed, discovered the feeling of community amongst them, for they were not lepers to her, but each an individual by name. Notwithstanding their swellings, scabs, discolourations, rashes, loss of hair, festering wounds that offend, with distorted faces and rotting flesh, Mother embraced them all. The odour of dying flesh did not hinder the giving of a new odour of God's grace. That of love.

She forgot that she was among lepers; she forgot the dismay of their wretched condition. For, she knew that by giving love she was committing God's will of caring for the nearly four million lepers across the country and give them a place to stay and not being deprived of love or being thrown out of this world. She said, "Lepers may be disfigured, but they, like us, like the rich and the poor, are wonderful people, and with a great capacity of love."

I agree, and Shanti Nagar is the manifestation of her caring and love.

I often saw the scene in front of Entally market repeated at other places in the city, different groups with different brothers and sisters, always playing the same rhythm and the beat of hope. That they would overcome some day; that their heart believed that they would overcome; that they would walk hand-in-hand, and that they would be free, and were not afraid, and one day they would live in peace.

Their rhythm and beat of hope was answered by this small frail woman. And, they received a place on earth where they found peace. No longer a curse to humanity, no longer an evil. No doors shutting on their faces. No harsh reprimand of 'Leave my home now, you cursed leper.'

A mother shunned by society, a mother turned out by her children in her old age, a father physically abused by his son, a son rebuked, a daughter with an unwanted child, a man and a woman with nothing to eat, a wife who burned herself, a husband who could not earn as much as the family wanted.

But then, how many doors have been closed to such lepers of the world? The greatest sin in this world is the lack of love and charity, the terrible indifferences to such people meted out by their own, comes from our own social system. For, we do not know how to give love. And all they needed was love, and nothing else.

The Loreto Order, which Mother joined, founded by Mary Ward and her epitaph says it all. "To love the poor, preserve the same, live, die and rise with them…"

From each of her actions I learned. I entered each of the doors that she opened. And I saw the wonder of her love. Mother's efforts on behalf of the poor came from a sense of duty of the conviction of God's merciful love, and the poor and the afflicted keenly felt the throb of her love. For those whom life had dealt with very cruelly were not deceived at all, as Mother was the first person they felt comfortable with. A Mother, who made them feel that someone really loved and took an interest in them. A Mother, that they all wanted.

And, all the doors that were opened by Mother, allowed all those upon whom the doors of life had been shut. Who, indeed, would like to be behind those doors that were closed for them? No one. Because they know which door they can go to and knock, for that door will be opened for them gladly. Let life triumph behind these doors, and let life begin. Always.

There were many difficult times that Mother faced in her mission of caring for the poor. Lonely and hard days were ahead of her during those years when she was all alone. But God's blessing and love does come in mysterious ways. A Bengali Catholic donated half his house, and Mother's Love Incorporated began.

The vows of poverty, chastity and obedience are the most difficult to keep and practise, for these vows are taken according to the laws of sacrifices. Yet another vow of giving whole hearted and free service to the poorest of the poor, was the voluntary sacrifice that Mother prescribed for herself and who ever wanted to join her mission. Many came to join her mission of love for the poorest of the poor and the house at Creek Lane could not accommodate the growing community any longer. A new place was identified, which became Mother House and the Head Quarters of the Missionaries of Charity.

Her mission grew, her congregation grew and her message of "Love thy neighbour" grew in the many hearts that felt it. And, they came to help her cause.

Mary Bella Mondal had no clue as to what would happen to her and her family when they crossed the borders of Independence. Mary Bella did not even know who Mother Teresa was. But, by the quirk of fate both came to know each other.

When the town "Shanti Nagar" was being built by Mother solely for the purpose of the lepers to stay and have a community of their own, the news spread like wildfire across the country. Slowly, one by one, the 'cursed' of our society turned towards the direction of that town. Till none were there to beat their rhythm of wanting. For, their prayers were answered, that they will overcome one day and live in joy and peace. A prayer answered by the small frail lady called Charity.

This group of 'unwanted' brothers and sisters of our society turned up practically every day in front of Entally market, and I after the evening mass always went to see them. My elder sister who was studying medicine told me that it was a curable and not a contagious disease. However, she mentioned that leprosy appears more repulsive and frightening than it actually is, due to its frightening visual appearance. This explanation of hers edged me to know more about this group of unfortunate brothers and sisters.

I came to know about Mary Bella and her father and her mother and one of her brothers. She had another brother, who I was told, was looking after the cooking and other chores, so that food would be ready on their return. The others were outcastes just like them and they had formed this group on their own. Mary Bella was not infected with this disease that plagued her family, and she was the one who did all the shopping and other purchases with the money that they received. The Mondal family were treated by the Sisters everyday and sometimes she said that a small frail woman came to see to their needs and who was addressed as Mother.

My enquiries were initially met with a little bit of resistance, but slowly the group, I found, awaited my arrival in the evenings. And, I came to know as to where they came from and their individual names. Upon coming to know that we belong to the same faith, the elder Mondal had a smile on his face. I was told by him that the Sisters were extremely fond of Mary Bella and that she had a talent for music, which was apparent enough from her playing of the flute. One of the Sister, on finding out her desire to learn, gave her a flute which was of the straight kind and easily available by the many vendors in our locality. Mary Bella started learning the flute and picked up the song "We shall overcome" from the same Sister who gave her the flute.

Mary Bella taught this tune to the others of her society living in the outskirts of Calcutta, which became the signature tune of their prayer. Mary Bella Mondal from Borisal gave the lepers of Calcutta a song for their hearts, and a tune to beat their rhythm with.

Shanti Nagar was built, the commune was being filled. Slowly, one by one they all left the world where they were shunned and abandoned and went to live in a new world, and a new life of peace and happiness. And, I did not see the group in front of Entally market again.

With the passage of time, I immersed myself in my newfound job and career, learning more about the truth of life and its hidden realities. Such was the tide of time when many things seen and felt had a different meaning of its own. Some brought joy and happiness and some sorrow. And, there were many others that I saw with awe. My elder brother's exemplary dedication towards his family members after my father's death; a friend's ever-present hands towards moulding of a young mind during its nascent years; the joy of coming to know the beauty of the seven notes and what it could create from a priest; and the wonderful presence of a woman's love through Charity.

And, I came to know that Charity actually begins at home.

Saint Augustine, one of the greatest Doctors of our church has given us something to dwell upon, which if we reflect will define the beauty of Mother's love through charity.

"O love, which always burns, and is never extinguished; true charity! My God, set me all on fire."

Music is a response of emotion and intuition and the listener is affected by its composition. The performance would either succeed or fail as rendered by the performer, and the creative processes that follow the line of a musical argument and to recognize the thematic relationship between the transformations of these seven notes is music. Though we may speak or write a million words about it, nothing can change the fact that in our life it stands or falls by its ability to move us, to stimulate us, to entertain, to delight, to bore, to perplex, to illumine, to arouse and to enlarge our capacity for a spiritual experience.

My experience with music was multifarious when I was introduced to these seven notes of life. The awakening of their messages changed the mystery of my listening. I was better equipped; I toned down to rise to music's challenge. There were other purposes too, for I did not want to be seduced by the sound of music without making an attempt to grasp its sense. Music and the city that Mother adopted also has that mystique which I saw as a child in the church of her fervent prayer, and it was music to my ears and love in my heart when I saw Mary Bella one day, many years later, after they disappeared from the streets of Calcutta.

The city of Calcutta has many joys and sorrows. The joys are her belongings, the sorrows are her sacrifices. As a Calcuttan I treasure those joys and immerse myself in her sacrifices, for I came to know during the troubled times of my city the immeasurable happiness it can bring and the unwanted tears. In a language that we do not comprehend, but a language that can commensurate with the intensity of its message of giving and loving. We live in an age where the entire currency of our life is in danger of being devalued; without any guilt we adjust our volumes to our convenience. It may prevent us from hearing the actual commandment of our life, but it does not prevent us to actually hear the existence that it so deserves.

This stupendous paradox called Calcutta has an exceptional school of music, and under their conductor's baton I have had the opportunity of listening to some of the greatest works of music, composed by some of the greatest composers throughout time. Orchestras invited from around the world played and delighted us; famous names have raised their hands to signal the beginning of a major work. And, in one of these recitals I saw that pretty girl, who was playing the flute in front of Entally market many, many moons ago.

The venue was the premier auditorium in our city, the occasion, the birth anniversary of Mozart.

The atmosphere was electric as the programme spelled many gigantic opuses by this famous composer. The gathering was a who's who of the elite of Calcutta and the academy was the famous orchestra from New York. The lights dimmed, the men and women in formal evening wear and the famous conductor from our country mesmerized us with the tunes of Wolfgang Amadeus Mozart. When after the intermission, when the wine-coloured curtain rose amidst thundering applause, I saw this pretty girl in a white long dress with a single strand of pearls around her neck, with a steel flute in her long graceful fingers, her hair tied in a tight bun, eyes shut, concentration written all over her face, play "The Magic Flute."

I do not know what happened to me sitting in the balcony that evening, but today that sight, which I have seen every day thereafter, washes over my mind, heart and soul with tears of joy.

For, I came to know that music can bring a spiritual experience and the strength of a Mother's love, all in one.

Mary Bella Mondal and her family, together with the group, disappeared one evening from the pavements of Entally market. Her family and the others went to Shanti Nagar. Mary Bella stayed back with the Sister who gave her the flute. She was sent to a home at Ripon Street, and her classes in music started at the famed institution on Wellesley Street nearby under the watchful eye of an Irish priest. Mary grew up in strict discipline and amongst laughter and happiness. She came to know all about the small frail lady wearing a white sari with blue borders and lines all over her face, and she thanked the Almighty for His blessings. Mary chose to fulfil her desire to be a flautist and became the lead in many concerts in the city and around the country. In one of her performances in Bombay, a renowned conductor spotted her and, without wasting time, took her under his wings.

Mary Bella Mondal from Borisal, a refugee of Independence, maimed by the hungry lust of mankind, shunned away by our very own, begged for death till a small lady in a white blue bordered sari took her hands into hers and resurrected her into a new life.

The green room was packed with congratulators and security. Flowers everywhere. I tried to squeeze in but the door was shut on my face. I waited patiently outside in that late winter evening. They all came out, the players of the orchestra. And I saw her, the flute player. My legs were so heavy that I could not move, my hands felt like lead and in that moment of paralysis our eyes met. She recognized me. Her lips parted and she smiled. I saw that her front two teeth weren't missing at all.

And, I came to know the true meaning of Charity.

Words fail me to express my gratitude as to what I have seen and felt and received from this small frail lady with a white sari with blue borders. But with a song in my heart I can only sing in praise:

"Nessum Dorma, Nessum Dorma
Tu pure, o principesa
Nella tua fredda stanza,
Guardi le stelle
Che fremono d'amore
E di speranza.

Ma il mio mistero è chiuso in me,
Il nome mio nessum saprà!
No, No, sulla tua bocca lo dirò

Quando la luce splenderà!
Ed il mio bacio scoglierà il silenzo
Che ti fa mia!

(Il nome suo nessum sparà!
E noi dovrem, ahimè, morir!)

Dilegn, on notte!
Tramontate, stelle!
All alba vincerò!

"None must sleep! None must sleep!
And you too, Princess,
In your cold room,
Look at the stars
Which tremble with love
And hope!
But my mystery is locked within me,
No-one shall know my name!
No, No, I shall say it when my heart meets yours
When the dawn is breaking!
And my love will dissolve the silence
Which makes you mine!
No-one shall know

And we, alas, shall die!
Vanish, o cruel night!
Fade away, stars!
At dawn I shall win.
All' alba vincero!"

Dhukhi Ram, Fatima and Mary Bella. Born into a world like any other, did not know what was in store for them when they uttered their first cry. Was it their fault to have been born at all or what we call providence. Fate or destiny, the scare of human trepidation has been etched in their minds forever.

And for Sita, John, Ramesh, Vijay, Carmel, Rebecca, Santosh and the millions of others around the world who found themselves in the same situation, never to live a life as ordinary human beings. These resurrected ordinary beings became extraordinary people who, with their survival, teach us a lesson, everyday, in becoming the torchbearers of a global phenomenon. That of the resurrection of life, in one's life itself, only by the sheer strength of character of a girl named Agnes.

The one miracle on earth even gods will find difficult to execute. To eradicate poverty.

From the soup kitchens in New York, to Shanti Nagar where wasting lepers wait for their soul food, from the Aborigine settlement in Brouke, Australia to Nirmal Hriday in Calcutta where the dying are given the last chance on earth to live and leave with self-dignity, she lives more than a frail woman in a cheap sari with blue borders. She was and still will be their Mother, and our Mother. A Mother who cared for her children.

I do not know where Mother rests today, other than the Sepulchre at 54A, Lower Circular Road, Calcutta, where her mortal remains rest. But I am sure her body, heart and soul live in the company of our God and in every man, woman and child whom she had touched. And, the innumerable many who are conscious of that touch, that will redeem their pain, by taking each nail, inflicting on her own body and soul, until the pain exists no more. Finally, free from the bars of a prison called inhuman life, free from the captivity of the fleshy lusts of mankind, free from the names of gods who do not descend, free from the tortures of mental agony.

Recovered from the illness of life's fearful fever.

Thank you Mother, thank you Blessed Mother for coming into our lives.

Unite in Prayer

Make us worthy Lord,
to serve our fellow-men throughout the world,
who live and die in poverty and hunger.
Give them through our hands,
this day their daily bread,
and by our understanding love, give Peace and Joy.
Lord make me a channel of Thy peace,
that where there is hatred I may bring love;
that where there is wrong, I may bring the spirit of forgiveness;
that where there is discord, I may bring harmony;
that where there is error, I may bring truth;
that where there is doubt, I may bring faith;
that where there is despair, I may bring hope;
that where there are shadows, I may bring light;
that where there is sadness, I may bring joy.
Lord, grant that I may seek
rather to comfort, than to be comforted;
to understand than to be understood;
to love than to be loved;
for, it is by forgetting one's self that one finds;
it is by dying that one awakens to eternal life.
Amen.

This prayer was written by St Francis, and was adopted by Mother as the credo when, Missionaries of Charity was instituted, and is recited in all the Missionaries of Charity homes, throughout the world, everyday.

In continuation to what Mother taught us, let us pray in our Acts of Faith, Hope and Charity, that this world will be a better place to live in, by all. Let us recite everyday, every week and the months in our life, so that in the years to come we are redeemed of our sins.

My Prayer and Yours

"Eradicate Poverty."
and
let everyone in whatever tongue
they know its meaning of,
Recite.

Authors Note & Acknowledgement

The names of the brother and two sisters of our society as mentioned have been changed to withhold their identity. However, they are well, alive, and are living a life which is their birthright.

The Sisters who are mentioned, carried out their individual duties with such perfection, that I learnt a thing or two from their dedication as a young man.

The portraits of Mother have been executed in charcoal, graphite point and dry pastels. My childhood scribbles became the basics of these portraits.

I wish to thank:

The Bible study and Catechism classes that I attended both in school and in Church, which gave a whole new meaning to the Acts of Faith, Hope and Charity.

My clergy buddies, who through their years of learning gave me the actual expression of defining Love, and a wonderful person who taught me how to express myself in the English language and will always be my big sister.

Entally, where I was born, for if it was not there, I may have missed Mother.

My Church, which has been an ocean of strength.

On receiving my childhood scribbles from my mother, I asked her what Mother had said to her in passing that day when I was introduced to her at our Church, St Teresa of Avila, opposite Entally market.

My mother just looked at me and smiled.

And, I came to know what Mother had told my mother.

Agnes Bojaxhui
daughter of
Nikola and Drana Bojaxhui
sister of
Aga and Lazar.
Born 26 August 1910
and
left for her heavenly abode
on 5 September 1997.

Requiem Et Pace